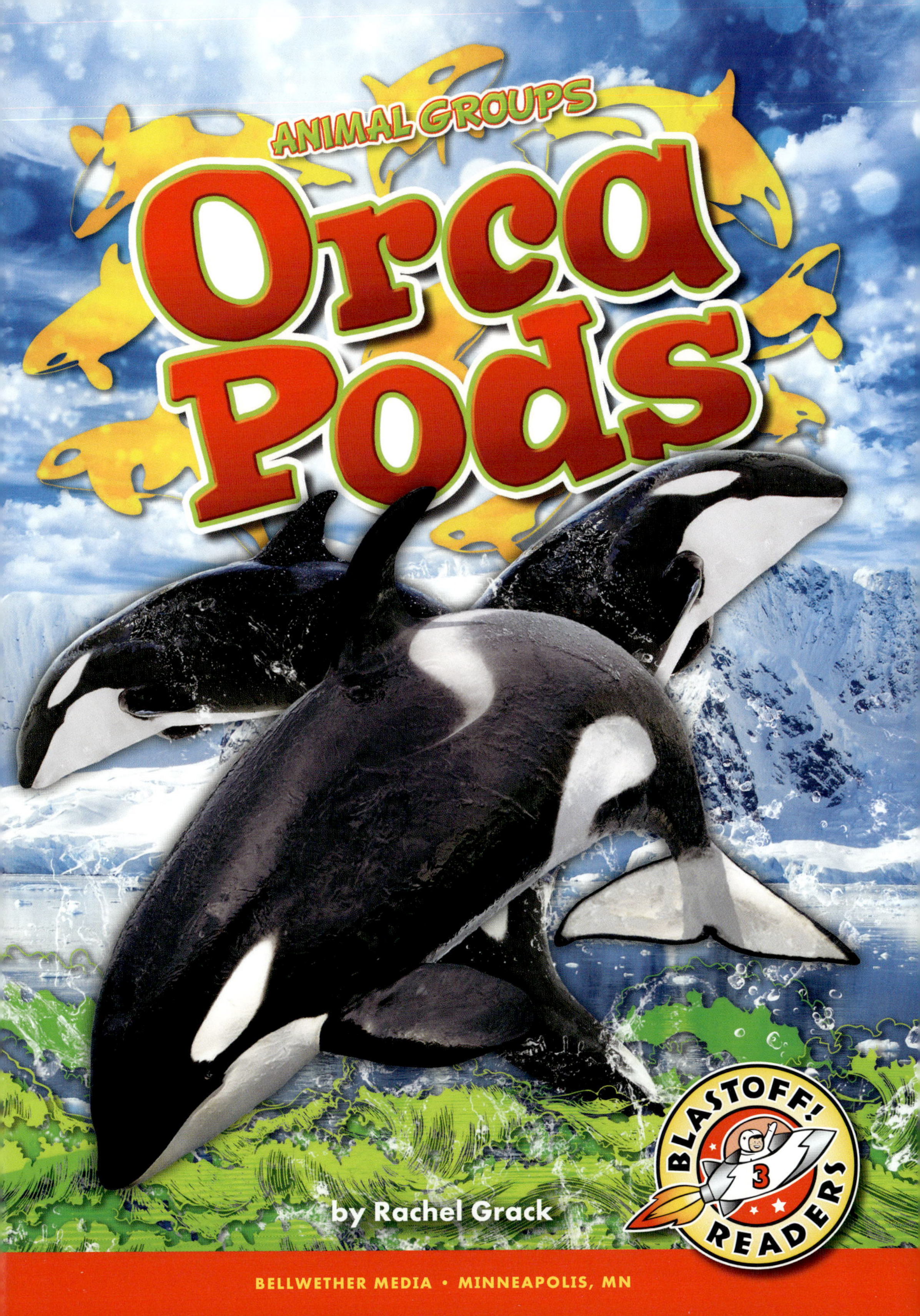

ANIMAL GROUPS
Orca Pods
by Rachel Grack
BLASTOFF! READERS
3
BELLWETHER MEDIA • MINNEAPOLIS, MN

Blastoff! Readers are carefully developed by literacy experts to build reading stamina and move students toward fluency by combining standards-based content with developmentally appropriate text.

Level 1 provides the most support through repetition of high-frequency words, light text, predictable sentence patterns, and strong visual support.

Level 2 offers early readers a bit more challenge through varied sentences, increased text load, and text-supportive special features.

Level 3 advances early-fluent readers toward fluency through increased text load, less reliance on photos, advancing concepts, longer sentences, and more complex special features.

★ **Blastoff! Universe**

Reading Level

Grade K

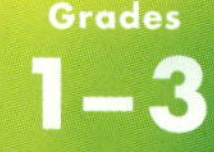

Grades 1–3

Grade 4

This edition first published in 2026 by Bellwether Media, Inc.

Library of Congress Cataloging-in-Publication Data

LC record for Orca Pods available at: https://lccn.loc.gov/2025018581

Editor: Suzane Nguyen   Designer: Brittany McIntosh

Printed in the United States of America, North Mankato, MN.

Table of Contents

Killer Whales

Orcas belong to the dolphin family. They have black bodies with white markings. People sometimes call them killer whales.

Orcas live in every ocean around the world. They are sorted into **ecotypes** based on their **habitats**.

Pod Families

Orcas live in groups called **pods**. Most pods have about 2 to 15 orcas.

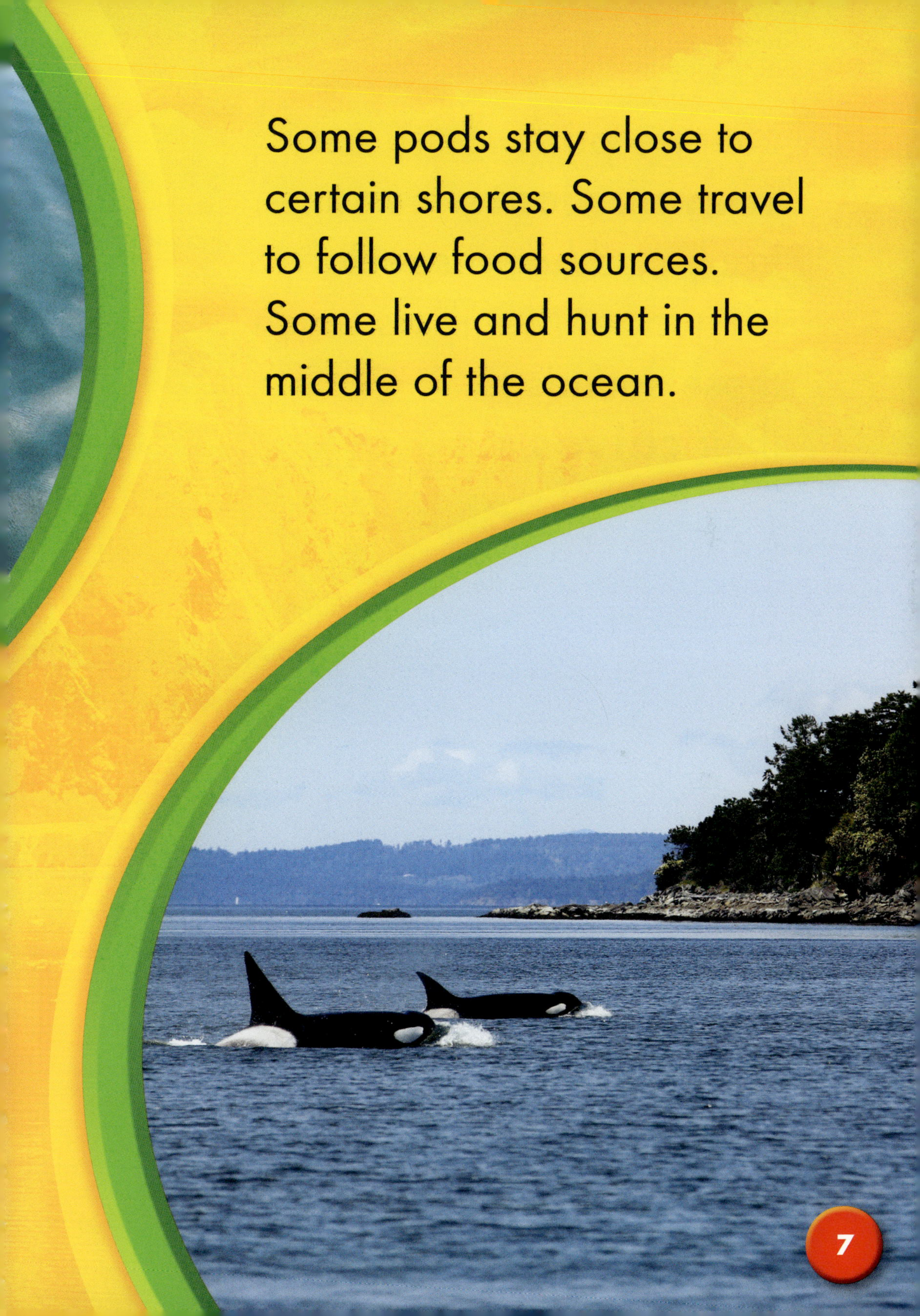

Some pods stay close to certain shores. Some travel to follow food sources. Some live and hunt in the middle of the ocean.

No two pods **communicate** the same. Each pod has a special language. Members teach these sounds to their **calves**.

Orcas communicate through sounds like whistles and **pulsed calls**.

Orcas whistle to talk to other pod members who are close by. They also whistle to organize hunts with other members.

They use pulsed calls to help find pod members.

Powerful Hunters

Orcas are powerful **apex predators**. The **prey** they hunt depends on where they live.

Pods feed on prey like fish, seals, and penguins. They can even take down sharks and blue whales.

Orca Diet
fish
seals
penguins

Orcas use **echolocation** to find food. They send out clicks that bounce off objects in the water.

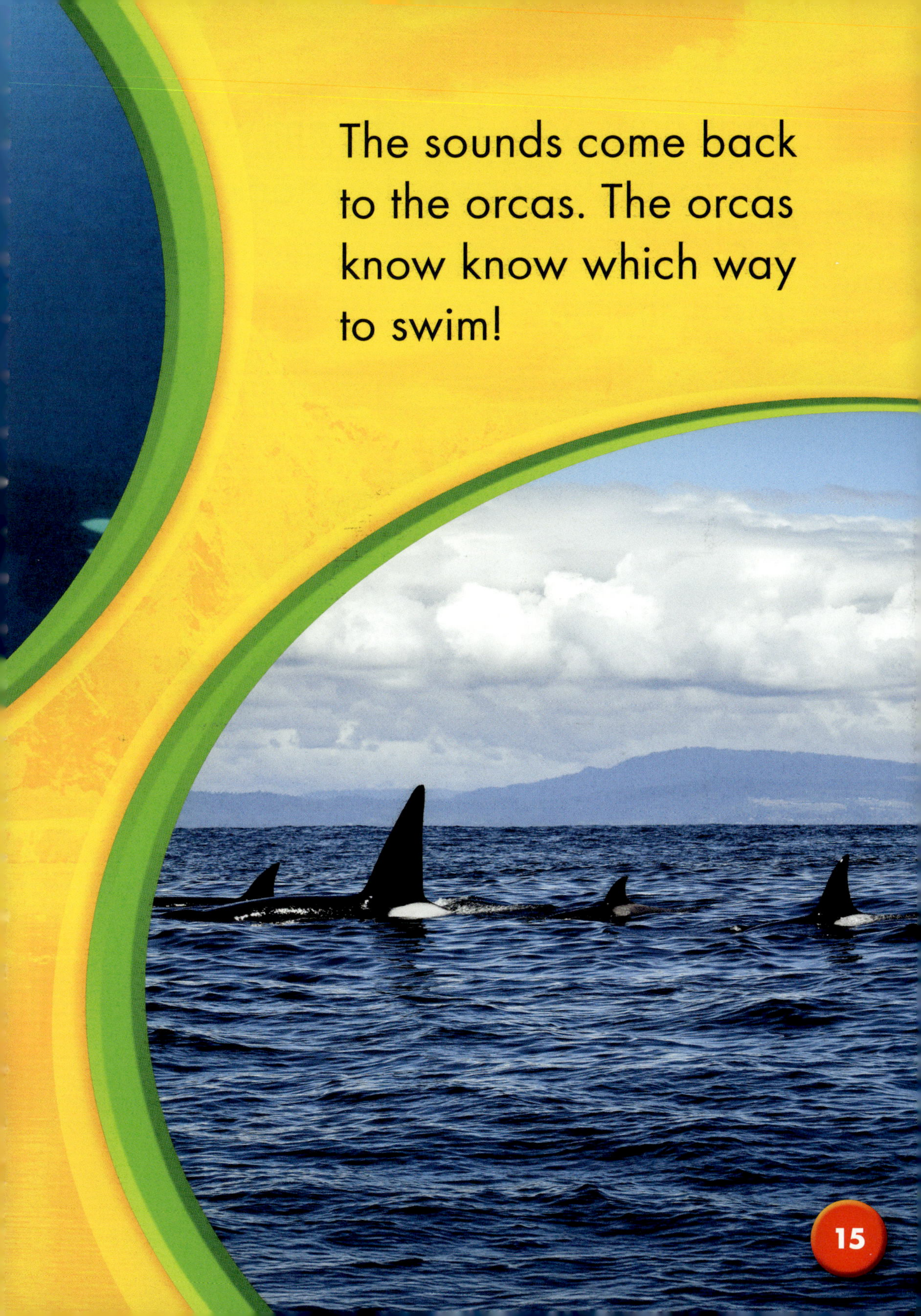

The sounds come back to the orcas. The orcas know know which way to swim!

Pods hunt prey in different ways.
Orcas make waves to knock
seals off **ice floes**.
Then, the orcas attack!

Working Together

charge the ice floe

dive underneath the ice floe

make waves with tails

seal falls off and orcas attack

Orcas use their tails to **stun** fish. They take turns biting large whales.

Raising Calves

Orcas only **mate** with members of another pod. Females have one calf about every four to eight years.

Close family members help the newborn calves come up for air.

The whole pod raises the calves. They teach calves important skills.

Pods have multiple families. They include several **generations**. Most orcas stay with their birth pods for life!

Glossary

apex predators–animals at the top of the food chain that are not preyed upon by other animals

calves–young orcas

communicate–to share thoughts and feelings using sounds, faces, and actions

echolocation–a process for locating objects by using sound waves reflected back to the sender by the object

ecotypes–populations of animals within a species based on their habitats

generations–groups of offspring born and living around the same time

habitats–the places where animals live

ice floes–large sheets of flat floating ice

mate–to come together to make young

pods–groups of orcas

prey–animals that are hunted by other animals for food

pulsed calls–quick bursts of sound that orcas use to communicate

stun–to make motionless

To Learn More

AT THE LIBRARY

Austen, Lily. *Smartest Animals.* Minneapolis, Minn.: Jump!, 2025.

Miller, Marie-Therese. *Orcas Attack.* Mendota Heights, Minn.: Apex Editions, 2025.

Peters, Katie. *Swimming Orcas.* Minneapolis, Minn.: Lerner Publications, 2025.

ON THE WEB

FACTSURFER

Factsurfer.com gives you a safe, fun way to find more information.

1. Go to www.factsurfer.com.
2. Enter "orca pods" into the search box and click 🔍.
3. Select your book cover to see a list of related content.

Index

The images in this book are reproduced through the courtesy of: Mike Price, front cover (left orca, right orca); Christian Musat, front cover (middle orca), p. 3; fivepointsix, front cover (background); slowmotiongli, pp. 4, 18, 20; Will Falcon, p. 6; Steve Azer, p. 7; MarkMalleson, p. 8; Jeroen, p. 9; Serge MELESAN/ 500px/ Getty Images, pp. 10-11; Tory Kallman, p. 11; Stephen Lew/ Alamy Stock Photo, p. 12; imageBROKER.com/ Alamy Stock Photo, pp. 12-13; Heather Ray, p. 13 (fish); Michelle Sole, p. 13 (seals); Fiq28, p. 13 (penguins); Wildestanimal/ Alamy Stock Photo, p. 14; Kim McGrew, p. 15; Callan Carpenter/ Wikipedia, p. 16; Sue Clark/ Alamy Stock Photo, p. 17 (step 1, step 4); Juniors Bildarchiv GmbH/ Alamy Stock Photo, p. 17 (step 2); Ivkovich, p. 17 (step 3); Agami Photo Agency, p. 19; Kertu, pp. 20-21; Marti Bug Catcher, p. 23.